*Not So Ill
with
You and Me*

Fani Papageorgiou

Not So Ill with You and Me

Shearsman Books

First published in the United Kingdom in 2015 by
Shearsman Books
50 Westons Hill Drive
Emersons Green
BRISTOL
BS16 7DF

Shearsman Books Ltd Registered Office
30–31 St. James Place, Mangotsfield, Bristol BS16 9JB
(this address not for correspondence)

www.shearsman.com

ISBN 978-1-84861-438-3

ACKNOWLEDGEMENTS
Some of the poems in this collection have previously appeared
in the following magazines:

Hotel Amerika: 'Notes from Bel Air'; *Blue Fifth Review*: 'On Closure';
Beloit Poetry Journal: 'The Jaguar's Wife'; *Guernica Magazine*: 'Headstand';
Salamander: 'Unhitching'; *West Wind Review*: 'Black Ice,' 'The Killing';
Verbal Seduction: 'End of Summer'; *The Hat*: 'The Blue Fox';
Dark Matter: 'There are forty-four ways to get over this'.

I'm indebted to the following books:
Entering the Stone: On Caves and Feeling Through the Dark by Barbara Hurd;
Being Wrong: Adventures in the Margin of Error by Kathryn Schulz;
Thrown by Kerry Howley; *The Empathy Exams* by Leslie Jamison;
A Lover's Discourse by Roland Barthes.

THIS BOOK IS DEDICATED TO ELINA KOUNTOURI.

"The important arguments are with yourself."

— W.B. Yeats

Contents

Here is a man, here is rich red wine,
inchoate years beneath the floorboards.
When you look up at the sky, everything is amplified.
Being wrong means having an adventure.
It is a journey and a story.

Consider the human need for war.
In the world of professional wrestling,
the men who hang around but are non-fighters
are known as "shadows".

Consider love that makes you strong
before it pulls you down.
If your heart had legs,
would it ever walk in a straight line?

Who wants to stay at home and be right.
They say you will know progress
by the number of people who are angry with you.
The sand on the beach chills quickly; the day is over.

Someone will spot you through the dim bar light
and the shadow will say, do you fight?

The question, heavy like a sugar bowl
pinning down a note.
We walk on air baby and
since we cannot jump
over two ditches at the same time,
we gamble.

So here. Take the note.

Travels Without You

You walk around the lagoon,
again and again.
The heart is a muscle.

What does the lake look like
Depends on who you are.

You know every lap of water by name
but there's a zero somewhere in your heart.

The lagoon is dissected by your thoughts
like a railroad bridge
and sometimes
as you walk at dusk
it feels exactly like madness.

You're not responsible
for anyone else's peace of mind.

Do you know the good years
when you're in them?

Or do they look like high doorways
that lead nowhere?

You can never know what
a particular connection is about
until later.

You keep a close watch on this heart of yours.

All the spinning, then the end,
relief.

There's a shadow on you
but shadows lead nowhere.

Maybe one day, you too will see something
you can't explain.

You need someone to push against.
Where have your hands been, you wonder.
You're watching for more shadows on the wall.
For their lack of blemish.
How do they survive when they're not like everyone else?

They say people get addicted to surfing
because it's impossible to feel depressed
when actually riding a wave —
then they could almost constantly have what they want.

You. Daylight banked against the blackness.
First square.
Lakewater darkens to stone.
Second square.
Joy without sorrow is mania
yet you only count the happy hours.

The light in the sky faint blue, the colour of ice.
In physics they call it the observer effect —
you can't observe a physical process
without affecting it.

Whatever it is, it can almost always wait.
In the mean time, what else is there to do
but carry around the capacity to worry.
This is what sunlight means to me.

There is a Roman aqueduct near Preveza,
a bone which belonged to a mammoth.
It's the place where a poet lived and worked.
He wrote in despair and then
for ten hours
he tried to drown himself.

So will you come with me?
I haven't seen you for a long time.

Who said that people are not bad
when they have plenty of room?

Nothing calm in these thoughts.
I walk along a band of pale blue.

My chest is heaving when I think of you.
I'm not big on endearments.

You weren't even mad at me but still,
you left first.

They say nine-tenths of poise is pretence.

In the Cartesian theory of vortices
all motion had to be circular
and all matter had to be capable
of further reduction.

Of all our games, we hold on to this:
the only one that counts is the next one.

It takes four-and-a-half hours
to drive from Athens to Preveza,
built at the entrance of the Ambracian Gulf.
There is a yellow sign on a curve
just before the road starts to twist and turn —
On the next 3 kms, fatal accidents tend to occur.

Then little towns on the edge of the sea
on the north side of the Peloponnese,
the green-blue of the Ionian Sea.

I began to count.

Suppose you threw a stone up into the air
and it didn't come down for a long time.
Suppose you just stayed there and waited.
Only staying power matters.
The Sphinx says to Oedipus,
the abyss you wish to throw me in, lies within you.

I walk across the lagoon to the spot
where the poet tried to drown himself
with a stone around his neck.

The sounds you equate with water.

The man who couldn't drown
because he knew how to swim.

The waves took him to the shore at dawn.
A policeman escorted him to his clothes.

You and I do not swim in pools
where we can see the bottom.

And so we go to Preveza.
To the Roman aqueduct,
the mammoth bone
and the man who tried to drown.

It's never just a place,
this is what life turns out to be.
The smell of dead fish, gasoline and salt,
never a straight line.

It is here that the poet Kostas Karyotakis found peace,
firing a bullet into his heart on July 21st, 1928.

There is a second round in everything.

Can today forget yesterday?

There is a story about a wedding in Naples,
where fireworks appeared in the sky
making the letters *Ciao Fabrizio*.

Passersby stopped to ask who Fabrizio was.
The brother of the bride, the family replied.

He had died years ago but
because they were celebrating,
they did not want him to think
he had been forgotten.

The sounds you equate with water and light,
which travels more slowly through it.

We walk past what used to be the slaughterhouse,
into the centre of the town, the narrow alleys,
the Venetian clock.

We have seen what we have seen.

The sound of heat.

Tinnitus is the word for noises
that some people hear in their ears
or in the head,
buzzing, ringing, whistling, hissing
and other sounds that do not come
from an external source.

Old men in white undershirts
hosing down the pavement
while women are talking across balconies.

Battleships.
It's that game where you make a grid
on a sheet of graph paper and each player
has one battleship (four squares),
two cruisers (three squares),
three destroyers (two squares)
and so on, then you have to
knock out the opponent's fleet.

We played game after game.

I sit up in bed and find
my wristwatch on the night-stand.
It's ten minutes before three.
There are beams running across the ceiling
and I count them.

There is a story about an early meeting
of the Royal Society in London
attended by the King
regarding a bowl of water
weighing the same with a goldfish in it
as it did without.
Then a balance was brought
and the experiment was carried out.
The bowl was put on the balance
and the fish was added.

It will be impossible to talk about me
without mentioning you,
said the fish to the bowl
and then the bowl's weight increased
by exactly the weight of the fish.

Horace said, change the name
and the story is about you.

Ciao Fabrizio.

The first people spent a lot of time
looking for food.

Frozen mammoths have been discovered
with bellies full of leaves and grasses.

The brain's ability to lay down memory.

What else is there to do
but carry around the capacity to worry?

In Melanesia whole societies
have withered away from weariness.

You wake up in the middle of the night
and lie still, eyes wide open
in the dark.

On warm days trout
like to hide in the shade
under stony ledges.

Iron ore,
once smelted,
becomes steel.

There is not one thing which explains us.

Edward VIII broadcasts to the British Empire
that he will abdicate.

While King Louis busied himself
with meetings and paperwork,
Marie Antoinette spent more and more time
at the Petit Trianon.

George Mallory's corpse found
seventy-five years after his death
on the upper terraces of Everest.

A thousand crossings.

The pure sex only lasts for so long
and then you must leave.

Freud said there are never only two people in bed.
How far do you take a thing like this?
Phone sex upsets people.

There's nothing to you
unless someone sees something in you.

In a cave, always look back.
Every few minutes, turn around.

Keep your mind on your homecoming.
Nothing looks the same coming out
as it did going in.

Remember, nine-tenths of poise is pretense.

Memorise the back sides of every boulder,
the shape of the hole you've just come through,
see the reverse of every angle of slope.

On the next 3 kms, fatal accidents tend to occur.

You have to know
how it should look going back out
so you can tell
if you're in the right passage.

Sunlight is the only temple.
Everything else is distraction.

In my dream you came to find me
to say goodbye.
The subways had stopped running
because of the storm.
No one has ever taken that long
to walk down a flight of stairs.

There are stories about sailors lost at sea
who went mad after ingesting salt water,
a song about shooting a man in Reno
just to watch him die,
footage from Watergate
with Nixon flashing the V-for-victory
from the helicopter on the White House lawn.

Your hands pressing on my face,
towards the temples.

Nothing is ever over.
Who walks that slow.

Time can be whatever anyone wants it to be.
I'm going nowhere fast.
You don't get to interrupt that.

Like in prison, whenever there is fog,
they count the inmates again and again

I'm checking to see
what is possible to want
and if we're still alive.

In 1951, forest fires in Canada
caused a blue Moon.

The only one that counts,
is the next one.

The Steel City

They keep telling you
in any life there is no pattern.
It's the mind which turns on itself.

Jesus is Lord and you know it,
says the billboard sign
at the side of the highway.

They seem to know
a great deal about yearning.

Leaving Chattanooga, tractor-trailers
blocking your view of trees
as you pass them.
You take everything personally.
You pass strip mall after strip mall
and then another sign
Tennessee welcomes you
Speed limit 65 miles per hour.

Crossing the state border
from Georgia to Tennessee,
there is a lost hour
but you're not thinking straight.
Sky, clouds, telephone wires
hold your bones in place.

And old iron bridge,
eagles flying over the highway.
The clock has gone back,
there is an hour you must relive.

Who is Jesus? 855-FOR-TRUTH

You head for Nashville at dusk,
the hard-to-see time
but once you're there
everything is shaped like a guitar
to better reflect their musical hearts.

Is life just a process of breaking down?
Should there be a law
that all clocks in public places
show the right time?"

You will ask questions
but they will be the wrong questions.
Like things too sweet,
the country-music element is amplified
rearranging thought.

Still, every third drink, free.

The next morning
you head for Graceland.

You want to travel both roads,
to make some trouble.

You want doors
neither to stay closed,
nor on their hinges.

The opposite of a profound truth
may be another profound truth
so you reckon
you can walk away from anything.

You're in the middle
of the mansion tour
when the air is sucked out of the room,
your brain broken,
your feet tied to cinder blocks.

Everything is about being tired.

You leave before the tour is over.

There is a rock garden
where Elvis is buried
and you sit on a ledge.

You believe something unruinable, inlaid in steel,
will one day summon in you a transom light
but you don't know how to wait
and there's no love left in this place.

It is easier to want something than to have it.

These are all horizontal trips
but wasting minutes there
feels like listening
to the ice in the river
breaking up.

It happens to everyone.

Someone is getting in a car,
driving towards you in the dark.

Life is no longer containable.

You must want something
to the very end
or else you're going to die.

Now the air is sucked out of the sky.

You cannot be that thing in the middle.

When you cross into the state of Alabama,
you refuse to be discouraged.

Birmingham was built around steel plants.
It is terrible and wonderful all at once.

Over the years the steel industry waned,
the plants shut down.

The difference between stillness and everything else
is that it's built on something, which feels infinite.

Your thoughts are like dripping faucets.

Even if you stay in a dark room
for the rest of your life,
you'll see that people never add up.

The end of steel means the end of certainty.

You could have joined the Peace Corps
or sailed around the world.
You see more monsters in narrow spaces.

This is not easy for you.
If you don't change,
nothing changes.

Steel suggests
a stripping away
of the inessential.

At night you meander the fringes of the city,
a hundred broken cars mending in your head.
You have to get fresh air, people always tell you.

It was John Bortle who created a scale
on which he described various levels of dark skies,
ranking them 9 to 1,
brightest to darkest.

Class 9: Inner-city sky
Class 7: Suburban/ Urban transition
Class 5: Suburban sky
Class 3: Rural sky
Class 2: Truly dark site
Class 1: a sky so dark that the Milky way casts obvious diffuse
          shadows on the ground.

You can see the steel
in the dark.
It is urgent for you
to get out of your life.

You know the days
will always get longer
after December,
that anyone who is being attacked
instantly recoils,
that looking for clarity
is looking for someone dead,
by shining lights across a dark lake.

855-FOR-TRUTH

You know wildness
is not only untrammelled land,
that you must learn
how to walk through walls
by envisioning what is not.
But you can stay in one place
longer than anybody.

How does it happen,
the giving up?
You once jumped off the Golden Gate Bridge
and you survived.
There is a second round in everything.

Upon hurling yourself into the air
you instantly realised
that everything in your life
you thought was unfixable
was fixable —
except for having just jumped.

The difference between stillness
and everything else
is that it's built on something,
which feels infinite.

Seychelles, ex-Bahamas

I'm the first on Earth,
second in heaven,
I come twice in a week
and once in a year.
What am I?

It has always been long walks for you.
Watching the sky
clarifying and darkening,
gray blue shadows
holding destruction,
a series of low concussions.

It is serious
or it is nothing.

You don't know what a mistake is.
What happens
if you stop wondering?

I will be undone
then lie on your breastbone
and you must do the same for me.

There is a French children's song
which tells the story of a small boat,
that set sail on a long trip in the Mediterranean.

I will never forget you, says the water.
Say to yourself, you lose them anyway.

Life is for wondering.

Getting to know someone
is like entering a mine
filled with eerie signs of past life —
an imprint of a fern
deep below the surface
can only be you.

Does anxiety have content?
Or is it is just an old house full of wiring?

Think of the Sun God's Sacred Herd —
they do not breed,
they do not die.

Is resilience learned?
The thimblerigger places a seed
under one of three thimbles.
He deftly scoots the thimbles around on a table,
then asks the player
to bet on which one hides the seed.

Don't people on extended bed rest
faint when they stand up?

The answer is yes
and for a while
and never.

A stripper works the men
looking directly into their eyes
as if to say that this dance is for them.

They say icebergs
are so deep in their element
that no matter how hard you look
you will only find ice.

Is it possible to be only one person?

We cannot walk around ourselves,
nothing brings relief.

Pain, the Marines say,
is weakness leaving the body.

As if we have decided to meet
in the Dizzy Teacups Ride
but what we have in mind
unleashes unbearable contradictions.

Don't be tractable, you say.
Be reckless.

We spin in gigantic replicas
of Victorian teacups
not minding the noise,
the bustle,
the bumps.

When you were a child,
on the wall above your bed,
there was a map of the world
as it was in Queen Victoria's time,
all the areas ruled by the British Empire
shaded.

Victoria drew much of her strength
from Albert.

There's a blurriness about you,
a space waiting for language
that calls up deep in me
something that has to do
with adventure and escape.
This is not tear-duct infection.

Telephone cables under the Atlantic
have snapped because America is moving
25 millimetres away from Europe
every year.

Mrs. Ramsay asked of her brood,
Why must they grow up and lose it all?

We're wheels made of rubber
and filled with air.

Always running up a flight of stairs
in other people's heads.

Heavy bones,
human eyes.

We can be pollen
preserved in lake sediments,
old cranes by the waterfront,
but nothing has to happen
for it to be life.

Every carpet needs a flaw
and a flaw like this one
could stop your heart.

Birds are crashing
into the horizon,
clocks go back,
then forward.

We sit across from each other
waiting.

Because you're always talking,
you measure sugar in grams,
the time of day in minutes.

So much of love depends on echo.

Every child is taught
not to stare at the sun.
Sun is to ice
as life is to blank.

We decide to meet in a bar
in downtown Athens.

If you want to make
a mirage go away,
you walk towards it.

There are fairy lights
hanging from the walls
and I know it's always better
to go fast with another person.

Even the name of the place
is full of longing.

This is where
the slow stuff happens.

You learn to live
in language.

Why do they say so much of pain
is resistance to pain?

A piece of string and a razor blade
may cast an identical shadow.

You feel your strength
is of another order,
yet in your chest —
the arrangements
people make for happiness.

What is the broadest water
and the least dangerous to walk over,
you ask,
and I say,
kill me now,
the dew.

If you unhook my bra,
I'll kiss you
so you will not be rushed.

Doors are just wooden separations.

The things you have lost,
shadows of fingertips through porcelain,
slowly amass in the centre of your sternum,
the same place you feel happiness.

It is best to do everything on purpose in life.
Someday you're going to walk into a bar
and not come out.

Desdemona says to Othello —
I understand a fury in your words,
but not your words.

I'll have the ocean
and you can have the land.

Five to six weeks
after the little boat sailed
into the Mediterranean,
all the provisions
have been used up.

Here's the lamp, here's the book.
There are no mistakes.

If you're upset,
think of the Dewey Decimal System,
of the rain queen
still living in northeast Transvaal.

Stare at the weave of the bedspread,
use your tea-bag five times.
You're building a world
inside your heart —
the smell of ponds and ditches,
dead leaves soaking in the canal,
the ancient cliffs of the river,
the insides of other people's houses.

You can start with dirty soap
and dirty water,
and with a little scrubbing,
end up with clean hands.

No one knows the name of anything.

Go to the window,
mist the glass.

If you wait long enough
everything changes —
water is no longer so heavy,
the well that went down and down forever
stops.

There are chamberlains
walking behind the Emperor,
carrying a train that isn't there.

The madness must stop
and sex is how you get there.

All the whiskey in the world
and then it seemed as though
anything could happen.

A drink with you,
any time, any place
you had written
but for years we didn't meet.

Fluids and minerals
stored all winter
in the roots of trees.

Is mental obsession
the evidence of love?

The way we answered that summons
was by following the water home
through a war of attrition.

Marines, Korea,
never talk about it.

Life means mostly
waiting for life.

Any given day a palace
made of elastic bands
where anything can happen.

In Athens every neighbourhood is referred to
according to its proximity to the Parthenon,
the way every detail of Egyptian life
was shaped by the flood.

We're meeting east of Kolonos,
west of Kerameikos,
the potters' quarter of the city,
northwest of the Acropolis.

What does it mean to be a woman,
you wonder
as you enter *Seychelles*, the bar.

As the heart grows,
it assumes a more vertical position
within the thoracic cavity.

Ideal conversation
must be an exchange for thought,
says Emily Post in *Etiquette*.

You never get anywhere with direct appeals.
You're so broke, you can't even pay attention.

In very deep waters
where there is no light,
the fish find their way
by vibration alone.

Would you ever dream of me?

Saturn ate his children
because it had been prophesied
that otherwise
they would eat him.

Make a lifelong mistake
so one day you can be right.

Heat never stays in one place.
You imagine his hands in your hair,
anticipation being a harrowed inner space.

Do you think more clearly
when you're a little exhausted?
Why ever travel in a straight line?

Some whisky is better than others
but there's no bad whisky.
An ache at the bottom of your spine,
a ringing in your ears,
never any endings.

That first burst of love and sex
that binds you
and the world is gagged.

Something safe is over
every minute.

Your body is mostly water —
a bullet going through it
is like a stone thrown in a pond.

Nothing is just one thing.

You think of the rescue dogs that get depressed
if they can't find any living bodies in the rubble,
of the people who hide in the ruins
and let the dogs find them.

There's something about inchoate beginnings,
about the need to be overcome.
How will you use up time?

Something happens while you're waiting.
Forget what you've been told.
Remove the sun, the rivers,
the routines and daily reminders.
That itch that you want to walk
until you can no longer be distracted,
that nobody is sleeping,
that you're almost home
is your whole life.

You don't know what it's like yet,
to give up on something,

For years you woke up early.

Doubt
is sleeping with a knife under your bed
only to discover the world is empty.

I wanted you to hold me,
to lay me down.

The desire to conclude,
a mineral on the edge
of something vast.

Nothing has a lid on.

When the sun dies,
the orbit of the planets will change.
The thing about planets
is that they know what to do.

Baristas in coffee shops
refer to an order of a
small, decaf, skinny latte
as a "why bother".

Life is units of meaning.
Say yes,
you understand.

Blood pressure is expressed
in units of millimetres of mercury.

Life is there to be wasted.

This is the good part of irreversibility.

One point defines infinity,
two points a line,
three a plane.

During the Second World War,
agents of SOE sent messages home
using deliberately misspelled words —
when they were captured,
they spelled the words correctly
so SOE controllers in London
knew something was wrong.

Wherever you go,
there you are.

When nine Russians tell you
you're drunk,
lie down.

About hypothermia they say,
You're not dead
until you're warm and dead.

The mind goes first.

Then you can't fill the gap.

Rainstorms are to sudden
as a man's hand is
to the small of your back.

There are only three rules,
which apply to the entire universe.
Everything has an expiration date,
everything is quantized,
everything moves.
Think about it when you wake up
in the middle of night
and go to the kitchen
to drink water.

So how will you use all your waiting?
The sun has not exploded
but is dying,
five million years left,
write that down.

How much do you know about exhaustion?

Raccoons will wash a piece of sugar
in a brook until there's nothing left.

That French song again
where they pick straws
to see who will be eaten up.

There is a legend about
why a lake shimmers.

An ex-king took out the eyes
from his people
then dropped them in the water.

Suppose you're allowed to have sex
with whomever you want,
suppose you can hold the tension
between two truths.

Then find a place inside you
and name it the lake.

Life means mostly remembering it,
like a hole —
the more you take out,
the bigger it gets.

The French song lingers in the mind
as the shortest straw
is picked by the youngest in the boat.
An end to waiting.
The cabin boy will be the one
eaten up.

Strippers are creating a fantasy.
You were stripping for a hundred guys.
There were men crowding around the stage
throwing money at you.

It was as lonely
as living with a man.

What would happen
if you just stayed still long enough
to solve the riddle?

You'd stand by the hounds
and blow the *mort* on your hunting horn,
the formal act of parting
to commemorate the death of the fox.

An end to waiting.

Dinosaurs didn't really disappear,
they became birds.

Seaweed can tell us
if rain is on the way.

Life is a long time.

Maybe that's not a mountain
but it's not your fault.

Can one win an elephant
in a poker game?

Is it any good using water
to heat the lungs?

Do thirsty people ring doorbells
seeking glasses of water?

Beautiful, beautiful.
Magnificent desolation
Buzz Aldrin said
when he joined Armstrong
on the surface of the moon.

Any dress looks good
in a heap on the floor.

Virgil tells us that
to prevent the men leaving,
the women set fire to the ships.

Mount Kilimanjaro is in tropical Africa
but it has snow all year round.

Focus on one thing that turns you on.
If you add sails to stone towers,
they become windmills.

You take me by the hand as we leave the bar.
When you open a jar,
a millimetre of air is released.
But first there is a little pop
because of resistance.

Holding hands
can sink ships.

Soak up on migraines.

Rinse your glass at the kitchen sink
before you go to bed.

This is how
you keep going.

One must love language
and what it does.

I spent hours walking,
thinking what it would be like
to be close to you in a dark room.

I wanted the walls to come down,
the dishes in the sink to break.

When the British Empire was at its height,
the sun never set on British soil.

If the earth had the qualities of a black hole,
its diameter would be 2 cms.

If you have good sex
it's three quarters of the battle won.

We only love others
for something they have,
never for what they do.

I've been waiting for so long
to be alone with you,
people say to each other.

Trains are the fastest way
of getting around on land
but when you want to see someone
nothing is fast enough.

You can't make sex go away.

Finding adventure in a single person
is like walking into woods
smelling of a thousand pencils.

I've had so much
disappointment in my life,
you said.

I used to stick my head
inside the laundry chute
and scream.

Don't you remember me?

Herman Melville wrote most of *Moby-Dick*
while looking out at the Berkshire Mountains,
shaped like a humpback whale.

You must agree with it
and love it.

If you're happy, you outrun entropy,
you're happy anywhere.

There are eagles and condors
high up in the mountains,
vultures circling the city
and bars to haunt.

But remember —
Nothing.
Lasts.
More than three-and-a-half minutes.

When men don't call,
the nerves in your neck press.

We will leave them
only their eyes to cry with.

Cancelled without prejudice,
says the stamp on your passport.

Jam tomorrow and jam yesterday,
the White Queen tells Alice,
but never jam today.

Of all the things you don't believe
it is that our capacity for compliance
is phenomenal.

Without contradictions,
there is no depth.

In 14th century Uppsala
two monks slew ninety-eight orphans
in a single night
and then did away with themselves
all because a blue fox had appeared
at a window of their monastery,
which they took as a sign that the Virgin Mary
was waiting for them.

Not only are we not the centre of the universe,
we're not even made from its primary material.

In the linings of our veins,
the desire to conclude.

You're holding me by the hand
as we're walking down the street.

I will be undone
then lie on your breastbone
and you must do the same for me.

Is pain weakness
leaving the body?

If all the sorrows of the world
were hanging from a tree,
would we still pick our own?

The answer is yes
and for a while
and never.

Desire is waiting for someone
to show up at your house
and keep going outside
to see if they're there yet.

Something to do with happiness,
a dam giving way by degrees.

There are blanks in any life
but tonight the bars are full,
there are bodies in the world,
mountains with long blue walls,
rivers meandering and
you don't want to go home.

At the end of the French song,
they're about to eat the young cabin boy
but all of sudden the deck is filled
with fresh fish jumping from the sea.
The young boy, as by miracle,
is saved.

No one knows the name of anything.

When the British Empire was at its height,
the sun never set on British soil.

If you want to make a mirage go away,
you walk towards it.

If I called you, would you answer?
You wrote.

There's something in your blood,
a wailing inside you,
big pieces of furniture
that won't come through a small door.

Who likes giving things up?
Only the moon has no weather.

Unveil yourself and things will be unveiled.
So how will you use all your waiting?

Behind the Roman general,
there was a slave whose job was
to stand in the chariot whispering,
Remember you are mortal.

People told you again and again
not to have expectations.
But how can you live
unless you're waiting for things to happen.
It has to do with not getting
what you want right away,
with putting things off.

Your ability to generate power
makes you the thing
you never stop becoming,
your worst enemy,
always your own mind.

Birds change altitudes
to find the best wind conditions.
The world will break your heart
ten ways to Sunday.

When it was discovered
the King of Spain had a lisp,
the population of Castile
also adopted a lisp
so their King wouldn't have to live
his whole life feeling embarrassed.

This is how we respond to trouble.
By taking everything to heart.

Our minds are story-tellers —
they want to come to conclusions
but part of what is exciting,
is not knowing.

To this day
historians have not determined
the exact route by which
Hannibal crossed the Alps.

So if I called you,
would you answer?

You and I are wanderers
so damn the world.

Learn to tell time
by organizing shadows,
find something trivial
and love it to death.

I trailed you for miles.
I even reached the place you left,
before you started walking.

If you stare at the desert long enough,
you can imagine the time
when it was all water.

A pause in the blood.
Like everyone else
we crossed the road at the lights.

A wooden sign, which read
Seychelles, ex-Bahamas
when we first entered the bar.

Is every desire a liability?
Love grows from lust.
In the event of fire do not use this lift.

If you want everything
to come together for a moment,
do first everything that frightens you.

You've got twenty-four hours left in this town.

That's all right, people say,
we'll look after you.
But for happiness you need empty space.
Could it be you?

This is round two.
With shadows under my eyes
I know *It's you*
Then I lay my head on the table.

So much of love depends on echo.

I will never forget you,
says the water.
Say to yourself,
you lose them anyway.

Once the waiting is over,
we're jumping freight trains together,
high-jacking trucks,
selling their merchandise,
burning the place down.

I want to see you.
Gravity is the best agent of resistance.
I have received orders not to move
but little by little
something has to happen.

I'm the first on Earth,
second in heaven,
I come twice in a week
and once in a year.
Catch me if you can.

       e.

Life is for wondering.

Notes from Bel Air

In the taxi from LAX
you stare at the sky netted with wires,
the sky which is so big
there's nowhere else to go.

It reminds you of Alexander
figuring out his horse
was scared of his own shadow,
then leading Bucephalus
onto the exercise field,
turning it around so it faced the sun,
its shadow falling behind.

You have the ability
to accept everything.

I had no interest in drinking in moderation.
And I still don't,
Hoffman told *The Guardian.*
Just because all that time's passed
doesn't mean maybe it was just a phase.
That's, you know, who I am.

You can know
and you cannot know,
all at once.

Your room a small cottage with a patio
covered in lush azalea bushes
and twisted vines.

The autistic man enters a lake,
sees a sign with
"No Swimming Allowed"
and drowns.

There are words
that are truer than other words.

Tile-thatched roofs,
French doors,
a fireplace.
Check, check, check.

Risk is a stone
under dark water.

You can prick your thumb on a rosebush,
bleed to death at home.

Cobbled paths leading to arched doorways
lined with palm trees.

A place of rest and secrets.

You're wearing a bikini
and two light cashmere sweaters
but in the winter of Southern California
anything is possible.

You form a template —
Accept exhaustion as a fact of life.
The mind doesn't like uncertainty.

You don't have to be permeable
to the way someone else constructs the world;
you're not a tea bag.

You're sitting on cushions
near an open fire with red wine,
watching the diminishing light.

Fire is a chemical process,
not an element.

Can you really catch a cold
if you don't wear a coat in winter?

Kenneth Turan,
film critic for the *Los Angeles Times* —

*When an actor as extraordinarily gifted as Philip Seymour Hoffman
dies suddenly, as tragically as he did, the mind goes into a kind of shock.*
*How could a person who could effortlessly be so many people
suddenly not be here at all? It doesn't seem possible.*
With his death, we've lost a true sage, a seeker of truth in performance.

The pool is heated
but still too cold for you to swim in.

You lie on a lounge chair
covered in sea-green towels,
reading the *LA Times*.

Your bones melt.
That is what defines you somehow.

From the North Pole,
whichever way you go is south.

There is a fountain
in the middle of a terracotta patio,
a cluster of Tasmanian fern trees,
the smell of burnt wood.

Would this make you happy,
you wonder?

You'll be broken open at the chest
and you stand warned.

Surfaces are olive green, ochre, salmon pink,
like in the South of Italy.

Lots of birds.

The morning light makes
the fern leaves look translucent,
splashed with lime.

Who likes giving things up?

*Philip Seymour Hoffman was a singular talent and one of the most
gifted actors of our generation*, Lionsgate Studios said in a state-
ment.

Man walks into a bar.
You're in the dark oak-panelled room
watching the Super Bowl.

Here is a man full of haunts,
trying to chat you up;
you cannot get enough
of what you don't want.

Alcohol depresses the working
of the central nervous system.

So immense, so without end.
La-di-da.
This is you.

He is a man of complicated loyalties,
a photograph inside a glass frame.

The thing about strange men in bars —
If you're stuck in the past,
they call it depression.
If you worry too much about the future,
anxiety.

Madame Defarge sitting beside the guillotine
knitting to pass the time
making a mark in her stitches
for each head that is chopped off.

Click, click click.

Philip Seymour Hoffman dead at 46.

Possible cause of death,
drug overdose.

Waiting for the autopsy
to confirm.

A syringe and frightening amounts of heroin
found next to him.

The way in dreams you leap off buildings
and it's still all right.

Gifted and haunted, reports CNN.
This is a thousand pities,
people are crying out.

You're soaking in the bathroom
surrounded by cream marble,
watching the news on a flat screen.

Your mind is playing chicken
with oncoming lorries
towards the centre of the earth,
your twisted happiness
and blank heart.

Your looks will take you places,
an old woman once told you.
You later find out that if you run to those places,
your joints give out.

You get into bed
with no idea what to do
with the rest of your life.

You wake up at dawn,
open your door
to get the newspaper.

It has rained during the night,
the air heavy with birds and sap.
You read the fresh edition of the *LA Times*
in bed with strong black coffee.

Actuaries and others who study risk patterns
pore over tables of statistics and data sheets
every day
in order to shed light on
what humans will do or fail to do.

It turns out the future
is not an overgrown house
with a hunchback inside.

The best predictor of future behaviour,
they say,
is past behaviour.

The only person who can make this go away
is you.

You have lunch on the patio,
an outdoor fire warming you up.

*The Polo Lounge has been the favourite breakfast spot and watering
hole for generations of stars and Hollywood deal-makers.*

One damned mood
all the damned time.

You order the Hotel Bel Air Original
Nancy Reagan "Chopped" Salad —
grilled chicken, smoked turkey bacon, avocado,
Meyer lemon vinaigrette.

You must be able to control your mind.

*The Terrace is particularly popular as it embraces the fabulous Cali-
fornia lifestyle of indoor and outdoor living.*

Man walks into a bar.
Shall the two of us run away somewhere,
he asks.
There are many places
to stick needles into.
The world is a chessboard,
a pile of bleached bones.
And you're mad at heart.
Your heart, a heavy
and leaden centre.

You watch your inner cables
for wear.

You know that the stethoscope
won't hurt you
but what can you do
with this sudden space in your chest.

When a stranger offers you candy,
you say no.

Anything I could get my hands on,
Hoffman said in an interview.
I liked it all.

You can know and you cannot know,
all at once.

In the taxi to LAX
the driver shows you Manhattan Beach
where Philip Seymour Hoffman
had an apartment.

The sun behind the windscreen,
a mass of pale yellow lemons under the sea.
The Jehovah's Witnesses say —
This isn't the real world.
The real world is yet to come.

The older you get,
the more every void is the same void.
In a museum you once saw a badge
worn by a Roman slave
who had tried to run away.
The inscription read:
"Hold me in case I escape".

In memory of
Philip Seymour Hoffman
1967-2014

www.ingramcontent.com/pod-product-compliance
Lightning Source LLC
Chambersburg PA
CBHW031321060726
47590CB00003B/1288